Keys to Understanding
Relationships

WWW, metaphysue . Com

mm
Universality on, TV

Scholecych

928-203-0730

888 866 - 4685

Keys to Understanding Relationships

Liberty Savard

Bridge-Logos *Publishers*

Gainesville, Florida 32614 USA

Relationships
Copyright © 2001 by Liberty Savard
Library of Congress Catalog Card Number:00-111529
International Standard Book Number: 0-88270-846-5

Bridge-Logos *Publishers*
PO Box 141630
Gainesville, FL 32614
http://www.bridgelogos.com

DEDICATION

I dedicate this book to my family members who have all caused me to realize that I needed to re-examine my beliefs, ideas, attitudes, and feelings about them. God has used my family to teach me how to love. I can now love them, like them, and even learn from them.

TABLE OF CONTENTS

INTRODUCTION

Relationships appear to be very important to God. Jesus Christ felt so strongly about them that He overthrew the religious rules of His day to seek relationship with people in every walk of life. This drove the religious leaders of the times to crucify Him.

The *Cambridge Dictionary* says that relationship between two people or groups of people is defined by the way they feel about and behave towards each other.

> *This definition best describes the focus of this book—how people feel about and behave towards one another.*

Relationships can be mutually enriched and nurtured to grow—or relationships can be soured with resentment and negative attitudes. Some relationships stagnate because of indifference and neglect. The outcome depends upon how people respond or react to each other. All good relationships are sustained by love and mutual enjoyment of each other, never by a sense of having to perform familial duty or by being emotionally manipulated.

Good relationships involve love, respect, courtesy, caring, trust, friendship, interest in others' well being, and loyalty. The words respect and courtesy mean: to set a high value on, to consider worthy of esteem, and to prize a relationship with another person. Bad relationships involve jealousy, manipulation, control, suspicion, interest in self, and little sense of loyalty.

The Living Bible translates 2 Samuel 2:6 as David telling the men of Ja'besh-gil'ead that he was asking the Lord to be loyal to them in return for their loyalty to Saul. Other versions translate this statement as asking the Lord to show steadfast love and faithfulness for their faithfulness. *The Living Bible* says a true friend is always loyal (Proverbs 17:17). *The Message* translates Proverbs 17:17 as true friends loving through all kinds of weather, and families sticking together in all kinds of trouble. *The Living Bible* translates 1 Corinthians 13:7 to say that if you love someone, you will be loyal to him, no matter what the cost to yourself. The *New King James Version* of the same verse says that love *"bears all things, believes all things, hopes all things, endures all things."*

Many Scriptures about trust refer to the words of a person, or of God, as being true and safe to rely upon. Trust also means to set one's hope and confidence in, to feel secure with, and to have no fear of the one being trusted. David said to God in Psalm 56:3 (*NIV*), *"When I am afraid, I will trust in you."* In many places in the New Testament, the word trust means "to believe in."

To recap these various meanings to this point, saving the attribute of love for later on, the hallmarks of a good relationship could be:

1. **Respect and courtesy: setting a high value on the other person or persons, considering them worthy of esteem, and prizing a relationship with them.**

2. **Loyalty: righteousness and faithfulness, steadfastness, loving at all times and through all kinds of weather, sticking together no matter what the cost, bearing and believing and hoping and enduring all things that come with the relationship.**

3. **Trust: words spoken can be relied upon, safety to believe in another, hope and confidence can be set upon the person, feeling secure with, and having no fear of the one trusted.**

Relationships

It can be hard to respond positively to another person in the face of strife, animosity, dishonesty, anger, and unfaithfulness. How should we respond in love to our difficult people? Send flowers? Buy gifts? So often we try to express love by doing something for another person, deeds that we hope will be interpreted as proof of love.

> **The other person may have desperately wanted an expression of love involving the mind, the will, and the emotions.**

When this person rejects the physical deed, we may feel our love has been rejected. Perhaps it hasn't been, rather the act was interpreted as an attempt on our part to avoid a more personal, mental, and emotional involvement.

If I really want to know that I can count on you when the whole world has turned against me, I don't want diamonds, I don't want a boat, I don't want money. If that is all you know how to bring to our relationship, what will happen when your money is gone? Will you be gone, too? If the world has turned on me, the expression of love I really need might be non-judgmental reassurance, just being available, or perhaps a long quiet walk with a friend.

The best list of love's responses is found in 1ˢᵗ Corinthians 13:4-7, which would probably be labeled as **List Impossible** by most needy, hurting, and fearful souls. The soul would cry, "Foul! Not fair! No one ever did this for me!" And yet, someone could reply that this is exactly what Jesus has done for you! The soul might then answer, "Well, sure, I love <u>Him</u> like that." Yet the Word says:

> ***"If someone says, 'I love God,' and <u>hates</u> his brother, he is a liar; for he who does not love his brother whom he has seen, how can he love God whom he has not seen? And this commandment we have from Him: that he who loves God must love his brother also"***
> (1 John 4:20-21, NKJV).

Hate is a very strong word and it can mean to detest and loathe. But according to many biblical scholars (per *Thayer's Greek-English Lexicon)*, "hate" also means:

- **to love less,**
- **to postpone esteem,**
- **to slight,**

- **to disregard, and**
- **to be indifferent towards.**

Ouch! Who has not felt this way about difficult people, particularly difficult relatives?

> *"Let us not lose heart and grow weary and faint in acting nobly and doing right, for in due time and at the appointed season we shall reap, if we do not loosen and relax our courage and faint. So then, as occasion and opportunity open to us, let us do good (morally) to all people (not only being useful or profitable to them, but also doing what is for their spiritual good and advantage). Be mindful to be a blessing, especially to those of the household of faith—those who belong to God's family with you, the believers"*

(Galatians 6:9-10, *Amplified*).

Charles Spurgeon said that we should never neglect our own household by only doing good for and blessing others, <u>while disdaining and devaluing those in our own homes</u>. It certainly can seem easier to show care and compassion to those you don't have to live with.

> ***But our families are God's earthly training centers for learning how to love.***

Do you sometimes feel like you and others in your training center are back in preschool and <u>somebody needs a nap</u>? God will crowd you into difficult, cranky, and irksome situations with family members, again and again, day after day, to teach you all how to love. He will accomplish this more quickly <u>even if just one person in the family cooperates with Him</u>.

If you were able to express true love in the following ways, do you realize that you would have wonderful relationships with everybody? You would probably become the most liked person in your city!

1. **Love endures ill will without anger or resentfulness.** *True. I have done that*

2. **Love believes in the potential of another person, rather than resenting current conduct.** *True I done that*

3. Love is patient, willing to wait for life change in others.

4. Love is courteous, kind, and ready to show favor.

5. Love acts upon, even searches for, opportunities to do good.

6. Love is never envious of others' skills, honors received, or possessions.

7. Love is never displeased when good things come to others.

8. Love never treats others with disgust, contempt, or shaming.

9. Love esteems others, assigning them value.

10. Love is never stubborn, cross, or contradictory.

11. Love never does anything out of order, out of place, or at the wrong time.

12. Love acts with respect, kindness, good will, and courtesy towards all.

13. Love never keeps scorecards on the sins of others.

14. Love never seeks self-gratification at the expense of others.

15. Love believes God's power to be working on others' worst behaviors.

16. Love never takes pleasure in mischief or hurt done to anyone.

17. Love initiates God's workings in others through right prayers for them.

18. Love bears, endures, and covers over all things, unwilling to expose others' faults except in the most extreme situations.

19. Love is long suffering even when provoked.

20. Love always looks for and believes in the best of others.

Matthew Henry said, however, that wisdom, love, and cautiousness could dwell quite happily together. So, if love can no longer believe well of others because of undeniable facts presented, love can be wise while still hoping for the person. Love can earnestly pray for the redemption of the worst person, yet remain cautious and apart from his or her actions and attitudes. Love responses are the key to turning difficult relationships into positive prayer assignments.

How <u>do</u> mere mortals bring these kinds of love responses to their difficult people? Especially since all of our unmet needs, unhealed hurts, and unresolved issues were birthed out of the difficult relationships in our lives? If you do not know how to dismantle your soul's stronghold thinking that is justifying your bad feelings and grudges, love responses will be very difficult for you.

> *Personal strongholds protecting deep needs and fierce pain will block God's love from flowing through you to others.*

Those stronghold have <u>also</u> blocked God's love from healing you. The keys to tearing them down are within your reach. Jesus said:

> *"I will give you the keys of the kingdom of heaven; whatever you bind on earth will be bound in heaven, and whatever you loose on earth will be loosed in heaven"*
> (Matthew 16:19, *NIV*).

These words of Christ contain powerful prayer principles that can completely revolutionize your life, and revolutionize your relationships as well. They first create room within your soul for life-changing attitudes and new patterns of thinking, and then bring divine empowerment into your prayers for others.

These prayer principles will make it possible for you to surrender completely to God. Obedience and surrender to the Word of God does require you to surrender all of your personal rights, grudges, unforgiveness, feelings of injustice, and hurt feelings to God. This is not to turn you into a martyr, this actually is the only way you can ever make room to receive your own healing. I can almost hear some thinking:

> *"Yeah, right. Give up my rights and defenses I have managed to hold onto so I won't get hurt even worse, and then I'll feel better? Oh, sure!"*

It doesn't sound very logical, does it? It reminds me of the first time I drove some 300 miles from my small home town to the San Francisco Airport back in 1960. I had never seen a freeway before. Driving south on three lanes of traffic (enough to scare me right there) below San Francisco, I kept looking across the other lanes of traffic to my left towards the airport. I could clearly see the airport to my left, but I had no concept of how to get to it. Every so often I would see an overhead sign, "To: San Francisco Airport," telling me to turn off the freeway to the right. I would just shake my head and keep driving.

Any fool knew (in 1960) that it wasn't logical to go the opposite direction of something to get to it. And since I could see exactly where the airport was on my left, until I saw a road that would let me turn left, I wasn't turning! My mind simply could not grasp the concept of freeway off ramps and overpasses—because I had nothing to relate this new concept to.

> *Loving, respecting, and favoring others who have caused or are causing grief is an alien concept to the wounded and needy soul.*

Getting even, striking out, controlling, or tearing down are concepts more familiar to it. While in exile and just prior to his death, Napoleon Bonaparte recognized an alien concept he wished he had understood. He said:

> *"Charlemagne, Alexander, Caesar, and I all built empires with force and domination. Jesus Christ built His empire on love, and there are millions right now who would be*

willing to die for Him." The only way Napoleon had known to achieve what he thought he wanted ended up leaving him without comfort, help, or love when he needed it the most.

Our souls are convinced that they know what is best for us, how to get it, and how to guard our pain in the process. They have reached these conclusions based upon input accumulated during our lives. At the mention of releasing those who have used and abused us, our emotions may blaze up in anger or seethe in secret while planning revenge. Or they may cower fearfully. Loving relationships with the difficult, angry, and dangerous people who have hurt and betrayed us? No way!

We were all born into an unregenerated state like the unregenerate Gentiles that Paul spoke of in Ephesians 4:18, *"having their understanding darkened, being alienated from the life of God through the ignorance that is in them . . ." (KJV)*. Paul told the Colossian believers, *"Once you were alienated from God and were enemies in your minds . . ."* (Colossians 1:21, *NIV*). He told the Ephesian believers, *"For you were once darkness, but now you are light in the Lord"* (Ephesians 5:8, *NIV*). We were born as tiny babies like little darkened, alienated lumps of clay on a potter's wheel.

Then human "potters" with darkened understanding and unrenewed minds began molding our tiny unformed minds, wills, and emotions. Think about that. We learned about ourselves, others, and God with our darkened understanding that was shaped by input from others' darkened understanding. That needs to be repeated:

> *We formed our most basic ideas about ourselves, others, and God with darkened understanding shaped by input from others with darkened understanding.*

Can you see how some of your most basic beliefs and ideas about yourself and others, especially God, could be seriously flawed? Are you perhaps driving down life's freeway, seeing the good life off to your left, yet you can't get there? The only directions to it keep saying to turn away from it—so your soul just keeps going.

Are you ready to make a turn that seems to make no sense, just because Jesus Christ is asking you to? If so, *"prepare your minds for action; be self-controlled; set your hope fully on the grace to be given you . . . "* (1 Peter 1:13, *NIV*). This is where the Keys of the Kingdom come into use. In Matthew 16:19, Jesus Christ said to the Church:

"I will give you the keys of the kingdom of heaven; whatever you bind on earth will be bound in heaven, and whatever you loose on earth will be loosed in heaven"
(Matthew 16:19, *NIV*).

These keys create conditions within our souls that open us up to receive divine empowerment to accomplish the works God gives us to do. The *Amplified Bible* says that the Word is always *"effectually at work in you who believe—exercising its (superhuman) power in those who adhere to and trust in and rely on it"* (1 Thessalonians 2:13). That says to me that I want to be like Super Glue on His Word. Stuck all over it! I have had to get rid of a lot of the slimy, gooey residue of the stuff of my past to lay hold of that spiritual Super Glue.

Many Hebrew and Greek words for bind have very positive meanings—to put oneself under obligation to, weave together, heal, undergird, hold, persuade, and cause fragmented pieces to coalesce and become one whole again. The word loose in the original Greek, *luo,* (and companion words *rhegnumi* and *agnumi*) mean untie, break up, destroy, dissolve, melt, put off, wreck, crack to sunder by separation of the parts, shatter into minute fragments, disrupt, lacerate, convulse with spasms, break forth, burst, rend, tear up.

> **These are strong words that a determined prayer warrior can begin to use to empty out the wrong beliefs and attitudes filling their souls with slimy, gooey toxic waste.**

Our relationships on earth need to be brought into alignment with God's already established will for them in heaven. Praying with these keys will refine and align your relationships that belong within God's will and purposes for your life, while moving out those that do not belong within God's will. In the Lord's Prayer (Matthew 6:10; Luke 11:2), Jesus prayed to the Father, **"Thy will be done on earth as it is in heaven."** So should we, with regards to every relationship we have.

The Kingdom <u>key of binding</u> that Christ has given to His people is the:

1. **steadying,**
2. **stabilizing,**
3. **seat belt, and**
4. **safety harness key.**

We can use this key to bind our wills to the will of God, bind our minds to the mind of Christ, and bind ourselves to the fullness of the truth of His Word. Then we can pray the same prayer for those we have relationship with. God must be in the middle of our relationships to set them aright. He will not mend our fences for us from the sidelines. These prayer keys are very effective in placing us up close and personal with Him.

The Kingdom <u>key of loosing</u> is the:

1. **self-surgery on the soul,**
2. **severing personal bondages,**
3. **slashing wrong patterns of thinking, and**
4. **spiritual warfare key.**

Loosing is a powerful prayer key for cutting away the ugly stuff that your unsurrendered soul wants to hang onto. This prayer key can also prevent any return of those bad attitudes, wrong beliefs, deception, resentment, and bitterness towards others. This prayer key can strip away the grave clothes so many of us wear into every meeting we have with others.

The key of loosing is very powerful in destroying stronghold doors that give the enemy access to harass you and those you are in relationship with. Our souls and their souls have carefully filed wrong mind-sets, unforgiveness, desires for revenge, and other bad attitudes. These "file cabinets" in the soul are infused with artificial life, and thereby guarantee that hard things that may have happened years ago are easy to access today. Few wounded people understand why just one wrong look or wrong word from their difficult people can set the pain off again. These actions of our difficult people can easily trigger memories that are on our souls' artificial life support system. And we feel abused all over again!

> ***The good news is that these memories are the only remaining power that our former traumas and our difficult people still have over us!***

Our souls' artificial life support systems can be shut down with these prayer principles. Our stronghold walls protecting our open wounds and justifying our bitterness and anger about them can be brought down by these prayers. This creates room for God to begin to make us whole. Becoming whole is the foundation we need to begin the repairing of the breeches between us and others. Using the Keys of the Kingdom prayer principles enables us to be healed, to obey His commands, and to be the restorers of our families and relationships.

"If you get rid of unfair practices, quit blaming victims, quit gossiping about other people's sins, if you are generous with the hungry and start giving yourselves to the down-and-out, your lives will begin to glow in the darkness, your shadowed lives will be bathed in sunlight. I will always show you where to go. I'll give you a full life in the emptiest of places—firm muscles, strong bones. You'll be like a well-watered garden, a gurgling spring that never runs dry. You'll use the old rubble of past lives to build anew, rebuild the foundations from out of your past. You'll be known as those who can fix anything, restore old ruins, rebuild and renovate, make the community livable again"

(Isaiah 58:9-12, *The Message*).

As you receive healing in your soul, your courage will rise up to look past the ruins of your past. Life change will come as you cooperate with God's empowerment.

You begin to cooperate by loosing the bad feelings, critical attitudes, resentment, meanness, malicious intents, and other grungy stuff out of your soul. Once you have stripped them out with your prayers, God—seeing how serious you are about life change—will begin to empower you to sow the seeds of that change.

> **With His power enabling you, you begin to talk, act, and walk in a deliberately opposite manner to how you were walking before.**

Here is what you do:

1. **Pray and loose the effects and influences of wrong thought patterns ("this will never work," "they are going to ruin everything for me").**

2. **Loose negative mind-sets ("all of my family members are mean," "nobody wants me to win").**

3. **Loose critical attitudes and negative words ("she just thinks she is so much better than everyone else," "he doesn't deserve anything he has, he's a bum").**

4.   Weed the thistles out of the "field" of your life by doing these things.

5.   Don't let your field lie fallow, allowing weeds to grow back—begin to sow good seed into it.

6.   Good seed: find something about someone to compliment.

7.   Good seed: sincerely affirm others for something they did.

8.   Good seed: encourage others to believe that greatness is in them.

"Sow to yourselves in righteousness, reap in mercy; break up your fallow ground: for it is time to seek the LORD, till he come and rain righteousness upon you"
(Hosea 10:12, *KJV*).

"Don't be misled; remember that you can't ignore God and get away with it: a man will always reap just the kind of crop he sows"
(Galatians 6:7, *TLB*).

The content of this book has been taken from my question and answer ministry on the Liberty Savard Ministries website (http://www.libertysavard.com). Anonymity has been assured by modifications of relationships details. So many painful questions pour into our office each week by e-mail, as well as by phone, fax, and snail mail. The Lord has helped me to answer these often hard questions. This mini-book on Relationships is part of a series of mini books with answers that I believe many Christians are searching for.

Put on your seat belt and prepare yourself to receive integrity in your Christian walk. In an old 1855 Webster's Dictionary, the word *integrity* is defined as "wholeness, the entire unimpaired state of anything, particularly of the mind." Personal integrity comes to you as an extension of being whole, of being unimpaired by former patterns of thinking that were impacting your actions and your feelings. This means you can finally:

> *"Let all bitterness and indignation and wrath (passion, rage, bad temper) and resentment (anger, animosity) and quarrelling (brawling, clamor, contention) and slander (evils peaking, abusive or blasphemous*

language) be banished from [me], with all malice (spite, ill will or baseness of any kind). And we [can become] useful and helpful and kind to one another, tenderhearted (compassionate, understanding, loving-hearted, forgiving one another (readily and freely) as God in Christ forgave us"
(Ephesians 4:31-32, *Amplified*).

People walk through life today with music thumping on their car radios, cell phones that seem to be surgically attached to their hands, and earphones from personal radios and CD players clamped over their ears. Does this not seem like a concerted effort of the enemy to so fill their minds with noise that they cannot hear the thoughts of the mind of Christ? As you bind their minds to His mind, they can make a choice to turn up the volume and block Him out. But before they make that choice, they might just hear part of what He is thinking about them. That's an exciting prospect!

A changed life, however—your life—will transcend any noise of the enemy. **The devil cannot blot out the power of a changed life!** So know that your God is wanting to work with you both to make room for change in yourself and to pray with integrity (wholeness that is unimpaired) for others. That life change in you will not happen just because you try harder. If your 'trying harder to be perfect' worked, why would you need God? We all need God very much, and I hope this book has given you some insight on how to work with Him instead of always being worked on by Him.

> *"To you who are ready for the truth, I say this: Love your enemies. Let them bring out the best in you, not the worst. When someone gives you a hard time, respond with the energies of prayer for that person . . . If someone takes unfair advantage of you, use the occasion to practice the servant life. No more tit-for-tat stuff. Live generously. Here is a simple rule of thumb for behavior: Ask yourself what you want people to do for you; then grab the initiative and do it for them!*
>
> *"If you only love the lovable, do you expect a pat on the back? Run-of-the-mill sinners do that. If you only help those who help you, do you expect a medal? Garden-variety sinners do*

that. If you only give for what you hope to get out of it, do you think that's charity? The stingiest of pawnbrokers does that. I tell you, love your enemies. Help and give without expecting a return. You'll never—I promise—regret it.

"Live out this God-created identity the way our Father lives towards us, generously and graciously, even when we're at our worst. Our Father is kind; you be kind. Don't pick on people, jump on their failures, criticize their faults—unless, of course, you want the same treatment. Don't condemn those who are down; that hardness can boomerang. Be easy on people; you'll find life a lot easier. Give away your life; you'll find life given back, but not merely given back—given back with bonus and blessing. Giving, not getting, is the way. Generosity begets generosity"
(Luke 6:27-38, *The Message*).

1

RELATIONSHIP WITH GOD

Question: *I am a born-again Christian and I believe in God, but I don't feel very close to Him. How can I have a more intimate relationship with Him? Should I spend more time in prayer, read the Word more? Why don't I hear Him speaking to me?*

Liberty's Answer: Just as believing in the opposite sex does not automatically make you married, believing in God does not automatically give you an intimate relationship with Him. Whenever we dig too deeply into the character of any human being, we almost always find faults and become disappointed. This will never happen when we dig into the character of God. Instead of denying that you have some doubts about Him, do your best to remove them by getting to know Him better. He wrote the entire Bible just so you could. Sample just a few of the things He wants you to know:

> ***"The word of the LORD is right and true; he is faithful in all he does. The LORD loves righteousness and justice; the earth is full of his unfailing love"***
> (Psalm 33:4-5, *NIV*).

> ***"Be merciful to me, O God, be merciful to me! For my soul trusts in You; And in the shadow of Your wings I will make my refuge, until these calamities have passed by. I will cry out to God Most High, to God who performs all things for me. He shall send from heaven and save me; He reproaches the one who would swallow me up. Selah. God shall send forth His mercy and His truth"***
> (Psalm 57:1-3, *NKJV*).

"For the Lord is always good. He is always loving and kind, and his faithfulness goes on and on to each succeeding generation"
(Psalm 100:5, *TLB*).

Sounds like a good God to me. Sounds like a God who could do anything. Most of us believe that to be true, some of us just struggle with believing He might do it for us. Some struggle with thinking that His love might wear thin by the time He gets to us. The whole Bible is God speaking to you, loving you in the Spirit, and nurturing you.

You feed your human body three times a day, and it will just end up breaking down in decay some day. How many times a day do you nourish your poor cranky little, pinched up, desolate soul with His life-giving words?

The more you read the Bible, the more you will begin to understand your God. He moved upon the spirits of men to write the Scriptures so that you and I would have access right now to how He thinks, how He feels about us, and what His character is like. His Holy Spirit supervised the original writing and has

3

preserved the Bible for centuries to make sure no would revise the truth of His Word that you would need right now. He wanted no humanistic revisions of His historical actions, His present purposes, or His future plans.

As we read the Bible, we must realize that we receive from it on many levels. We are always being strengthened, encouraged, and enlightened in the present. At the same time, the Word is being stored in our minds to surface and click into place when we read another Scripture or have a particular experience even years into the future.

Question: *In 1994, I was working in a very good job with the government, when I thought I heard the words, "August 12th is your last day, you have a new boss." Within four weeks, I resigned from my job and began a Christian travel agency. Since that time we have lost the agency, our home, our car, and my spouse and I are living with my brother and his wife. How could I have been so wrong? Did I jump too fast?*

Liberty's Answer: There are times when we do hear from God, but our souls leap to act upon their limited understanding. This can cause us to get ahead of God's <u>easiest pathway</u> to the fulfillment of the purpose for His word to us. Sometimes we hear the voice of our souls' unmet needs and unresolved issues (which can be harder to recognize than the voice of the devil), and we launch our own agendas. Years ago when everyone in the church was worrying about "wild fire" springing up in the services (I'm not even sure what that meant, perhaps someone getting too radical or manifesting soulish things?), my wonderful old pastor said, "I would rather try to redirect a wild fire than resurrect dead embers and ashes!"

I think a well-intentioned mistake in trying to do what God might have said is better than hunkering down in a corner and always playing it safe. I tell young ministers who feel discouraged, "If you aren't making any mistakes in your ministry efforts, you are probably not stepping far enough out in faith. You can learn a lot from a mistake."

One pastor told of racing his very pregnant wife to the hospital in their little Volkswagen Beetle, when he was forced to squeal to a stop at a red light. Impatiently, he kept trying to twist the steering wheel back and forth, but found it quite stiff and resistant while the car was sitting still. Volkswagen Beetles did not have power steering in the mid 70's. The light changed and he took his foot off the brake and let the clutch out, and the Beetle began to move forward. Immediately the steering wheel became easier to turn. He felt God was saying that He could do little with him when he had his foot on the brake of his life and was sitting still. But when he began to move slowly forwards, God could more easily turn him to the left or right, or stop him.

You tried to take a step of faith. God will not waste one jot or tittle of what you have been through, even to the refining of possible hidden motives in your soul. I've long been one who stepped off cliffs for God— whether He had asked me to or not. God often doesn't tell me what is coming in my life because I don't just meet Him there, I try to beat Him there! But I've finally learned to wait (most of the time), sometimes even enjoying not having to figure out the details of how He will bring something to pass.

> *He knows what He is doing, He controls the realm we live in; and He knows how to bring time, provision, and everyone else involved all together perfectly.*

It took me a long time and lot of loosing of preconceived wrong ideas and wrong beliefs on my part to learn that God is never in a hurry. In fact, I believe His "clock" has no hands on it at all. Still, don't ever let the soooo-spiritual phrase, "I'm just waiting on God," be an excuse for inaction (or laziness).

In the Word, God tells us to ask and seek, to pursue knowing His will. There is no verse that says, "Follow your nose wherever it leads you, and God will get your attention when He needs you." Which would seem to be the most desirable approach to knowing the will and timing of God? Enthusiastically pressuring God over and over, "Now, Lord? Now?" Or, "Let me know when you want me, Lord, I'll be over here snoozing until you open all the doors for me."

The only way you miss God's opportunities are through disobedience, rebelliousness, fear, doubt, and presumption.

I don't think you ever miss one of God's opportunities through the honest mistake of being an eager beaver. The most sincere efforts (even when misguided and off kilter) to finding God's opportunities will eventually lead you into His will. And He will effectively use every scraped knee, bruised shin, and goose egg on your head to teach you positive things along the way.

He wants you to be willing to walk with Him into the unknown. He is not worried that any of His windows of opportunity will close while you are learning to do that. You may have moved forward too quickly towards

7

what you believed was a divine opportunity. You may have been responding to your own soul's desires to get on with exciting plans. Or, you may have just enrolled yourself in the School of Prerequisites to Your Destiny! Whichever, I believe you did what you did because of a desire to do the will of God.

Have you blown your divine window of opportunity? Not at all! You've just had to attend a few sessions of Remedial Walking in the Spirit 101 in the School of Prerequisites. I would say, after reading what has happened, that you may have even been on the accelerated track!

> *God will use everything you have done (right or wrong) to train you to hear His voice and walk in His timing in future situations—if you are willing to see the results through His eyes.*

This may have been an extremely important and necessary lesson you needed to learn at your present level of walking in the Spirit. What has happened may be directly related to your learning how to walk in the Spirit on a higher level because of a major opportunity coming your way! He will use each stone you trip over as a disguised nugget of gold for your destiny training.

God is ready to move on, but you need to determine that you are ready to let Him show you how to apply what you have learned.

Question: *Thanks and praise to God for your great books and also excellent web page! I have been struggling with strongholds for about eight years. I know they are strongholds after reading all three of your books last week. I am loosing a lot of things and have seen noticeable changes in my relationships. But my major symptoms (fleshly pleasure—mostly food) stemming from some unhealed hurts are still strong. Do I need some high powered loosing or is it a matter of binding something I haven't yet bound (or loosed), or being more persistent?*

Liberty's Answer: The unsurrendered soul convinces the body that there are physical behaviors that will help to ease the soul's feelings of neediness, pain, and doubt. This can be manifested in eating disorders, chemical dependence, inappropriate sexual acting out, getting into wrong relationships, and so many other things the mind instructs the body to do.

> **The mind sends out directives or impulses to the body to enact a behavior capable of blocking out the soul's distress. These wrong directives, impulses, travel from the brain to the body over neural pathways.**

The more the behavior seems to ease the soul's pain and distress, the more the same wrong directives are sent. These neural pathways become etched into the brain, and the mind turns to them again and again for temporary natural relief.

Try praying this way for a few weeks: Bind your mind to the mind of Christ. Then loose the wrong cues, directives, and signals your brain is sending to the body whenever your soul feels anxious or emotionally overwhelmed. Loose, rip, and tear up the wrong neural pathways etched in the brain. Then use the Word, declaring Scriptures aloud, to receive God's peace and grace, building new pathways for permanent godly relief!

If you pray to loose worry about money, and you feel tempted to use food to chemically pacify anxiety, then personalize a favorite Scripture, turning it into a prayer, and recite it or even sing it. Make up a new melody, or sing them to the tune of a favorite praise song or even a golden oldie from your younger days.

Believe it or not, I think this fits to Harry Bellefonte's Calypso banana boat song that went "Dayo, daaayo, daylight come and I want to go home . . . . ":

> *"I bind my mind and my thoughts to your will, Lord, and to the mind of Christ. I will keep my life free from the love of money and be content with what I have, because God has said, 'Never will I leave you or forsake you.' So I will say with confidence, 'The Lord is my helper; I will not be afraid'"*
>
> (from Hebrews 13:5-6, *NIV*).

If you are feeling fearful, and thinking of some wrong behavior that could pacify your fears, pray and loose fear and then personalize and recite and sing this Scripture prayers:

> *"I bind my mind to the mind of Christ, and I loose emotional fear, and the deception that I am not important to God, from my soul. For Jesus said are not two sparrows sold for a copper coin? And not one of them falls to the*

11

> **ground apart from my Father's will.
> But the very hairs of my head are all
> numbered. I will not fear therefore;
> because God's own Word says that I
> am of more value than many
> sparrows"**
>
> (from Matthew 10:2, *NKJV*).

If you feel inadequate and want to back out of a great opportunity the Lord has brought to you, pray and loose old patterns of thinking and wrong mind sets, and then personalize and recite and sing this Scripture prayer:

> **"I bind myself to the truth of the
> Word, and its ability to work
> supernaturally within me. Therefore,
> I affirm that I can indeed do
> everything God asks me to do with the
> help of Christ, which strengthens me
> and gives me power"**
>
> (from Philippians 4:13, *TLB*).

Please also pray the Breaking Soul Power Prayer on page 30 of my second book, ***Breaking the Power*** (also found in the mini book on Soul Power), every day for 30 days. That will bring about a major change, as well. Let me know how you are doing.

Question: *How do Christians know God's voice? For example, when I travel and I speak to my natural Dad over the phone, I know his voice—wherever I am. When our Heavenly Father speaks to us, how do we know it is Him? How do we LEARN to recognize His voice?*

Liberty's Answer: God truly does want us to hear His voice. He does not play games with us, test us to see if we are spiritual enough, or run us through a maze to see if we are smart enough to hear His voice. I believe He just speaks to us whenever we stop and quiet ourselves to listen. We have a lot of stuff going on in our minds and our emotions, "stuff" that seems quite capable of stirring up static between us and the voice of God.

> *I don't believe God raises His voice to get past the static, I believe He wants us to stop the static.*

We do this by loosing (cutting, slashing, severing) all of the frantic patterns of thinking about those things that keep crying for our attention: worry, fear, duty, anxiety, need, etc.

We also help clear up this static when we bind our minds to the mind of Christ, and loose any wrong belief we have that it is hard to hear from God. It is only hard when <u>we</u> don't unclutter our communication lines.

> *I suppose God could yell at us and get our attention. But if you were wanting an intimate moment with someone who wouldn't stop watching television and talking on a cell phone, would yelling at him or her encourage an intimate moment?*

Try the simple steps above, and ask God to show you more. He wants you to know His voice.

Question: *Thank you for your work and all of the effort you put forth to help others. My question is about relationships, both with people and with God. I understand that I need Jesus in charge of my life, and I need to live according to His will. Yet I still make choices that I know are not in keeping with His will, but stem from wanting my will. Only when things really get tough am I likely to spend more time in prayer.*

Liberty's Answer: What you have said is consistent with the actions of a strong soul creating diversions to distract you from staying with a prayer plan that works. Praying only when things get really tough (I call that panic praying) is not nearly as effective as regular prayer communication with God.

> *If someone you cared deeply about only came around you when they were in trouble and needed something, it would be very hard to establish a healthy relationship with that person. I don't think God necessarily feels used when we do that, but I do know it does nothing to deepen our relationship with Him. You are seeing prayer as an emergency resource, rather than a way of spending time with the Lord.*

If you really want to jump start things with God, begin to pray the page 30 prayer in *Breaking the Power* (also found in the mini book on Soul Power). People who go to counselors who are using these principles have prayed that prayer for 30 days at their counselors' request. After the 30 days were up and the counselors wanted to start working on issues that had been too painful before, again and again they say their clients replied: "I don't feel that is much of a problem anymore."

Question: *I seem to have a great need for companionship, a painful need to be understood, and an embarrassing desire for acceptance and approval. My husband is not very good at meeting these needs. I know that the answer is not to pursue other relationships that are not in keeping with God's will. I would like to believe that a relationship with Jesus could meet this need. However, when I do pray and talk to Jesus, I never seem to get a satisfying response. I don't sense any connection with Him.*

Liberty's Answer: This unsatisfied feeling goes back to unmet needs that have probably been in your soul for a very long time. Down deep in your heart (soul), you know you will never get such needs met by another human being. Only the Lord can meet them. That is why you are not getting relief and satisfaction from the relationships you do have. You need to consistently pray and bind your mind to the mind of Christ while loosing the defensive walls and stronghold thinking that you have layered over these old needs and hurts.

I believe there is actually a fear of intimacy behind your neediness. You made yourself vulnerable to others in the past who took advantage of you. Have you ever made any personal vows that you would never let anyone get close enough to take advantage of you again? If so, you need to loose them. Then ask God to forgive you for trying to protect yourself in this way.

Tell Him you are ready to tear down every self-defense you have, loosing all self-protective devices out of your soul. Tell Him that you are going to fight through the jungle of your soul's defense systems to come before Him stripped of all of your armor, buck-naked even, without so much as a fig leaf to hide behind. God is only waiting for a voluntary invitation from you to invite Him closer to love you and heal you.

Question: *I believe that God loves everyone and that includes me. Is it wrong for me to want God to make this more personal for me? Is it wrong to want to feel emotionally loved, comforted, and secure?*

Liberty's Answer: No, it is not. Do not discount your feelings, because God gave you those emotions. They give color and flavor to your life, sort of like fine spices. But if you allow even a fine spice to dominate a recipe, it ruins it. God absolutely wants your relationship with Him more personal. He is not the one creating the barriers to this, you are. But that is the good news, not the bad news—because you have the means of destroying those barriers with the binding and loosing prayers.

Tell God that you are going to tear down your strongholds and let Him into your soul to heal you. Keep doing this, even when you think you are okay. Don't let your soul dupe you into believing that a little prayer goes a long way, so you should be a big boy now. Don't stop until God heals you and you know it!

2

RELATIONSHIP WITH PARENTS

Question: *I always tried to honor my parents, but they were so critical of everything I ever did. And now my children are extremely critical of me. I feel like I can't win. I feel like no one accepts anything I say or do. What am I missing here?*

Liberty's Answer: You say that your parents and your children are extremely critical of you. I think you are overlooking the missing link here—yourself. Your children probably did not learn to be critical from their grandparents, they probably learned it from you. The pain you feel from this has caused you to see only their criticism towards you, but I would imagine this is a pattern engrained in all of you. Perhaps for generations. These are what I call generational bondage attitudes and patterns of wrong thinking.

This is an exciting prayer assignment for you, because you have an opportunity here to break this bondage off of your family. Write down, recite, pray, and even sing the following prayer:

> *"I bind my mind to your mind, Jesus, and I ask you to speak your thoughts into my soul as I loose, tear off, and shatter the hold of the stuff that has it all clogged up. For every square inch that is freed up in me, pour in your grace, mercy, and love.*
>
> *I loose all wrong generational bondage thinking patterns from myself, from my parents, and from my children. Please teach us how to develop new patterns of thinking and speaking to each other. I commit to you that I will not only loose my old wrong attitudes and patterns of thinking and*

speaking, but I will replace them with good seed sown for a harvest of harmony and love in my family.

I will be the first one to sow these good seeds. I will speak words of encouragement, I will speak words of nurturing, I will speak words of affirmation, and I will speak words of love. I will act encouraged, I will do deeds that comfort, I will create new patterns of thinking in myself. I ask that you will not let me, or anyone in my family, get away with just common words or silence either. I ask you to constantly remind us to speak and act according to your love and your truth.

Show us when we are not succeeding in this, so that we can change and belong to the truth. Show me and show my family members how our hearts can be at rest in your presence, no longer condemning us. You, God, are greater than our hearts, and you know everything"

(from 1 John 3:18-19, *NIV*).

21

God speaks something very powerful in Isaiah 45:19 (*Amplified*) about how He sees the truth of His words. He says:

> *"I have not spoken in secret, in a corner of the land of darkness; I did not call the descendants of Jacob (to a fruitless service) saying, Seek Me for nothing (but promised them a just reward). I the Lord speak righteousness—the truth (trustworthy, straightforward correspondence between deeds and words). I declare the things that are right."*

We must loose the old ways we have communicated with others, and then we must speak differently by faith. We must believe that God will empower us in new ways of communicating with each other. If water is contaminated, adding pure water to it doesn't help—you just have more water that is still contaminated. So it is with our souls. We must empty them of the waste of years lived in pain, and let God wash them clean. Then we begin to fill them with the pure water of the Word, that we will be like fresh gurgling streams.

Question: *I lost my father three years ago, and I feel as though a part of me died with my Dad. He was the only person I remember really feeling safe with. It's like I went into a deep, deep cave, and I am just now trying to find my way out. People have always viewed me as this really strong man, and I guess I've put on a good face. But no one knows that I'm hurting and so torn up emotionally. I had a childhood full of hurtful experiences and rejection that cause me to struggle with opening up and embracing other people. I could only open up to my Dad. All the feelings and emotions I thought I was free from are back—loneliness, rejection, despair, lost direction, and now the unrelenting grief. Just when I thought I had reached some level of security and maturity in Christ, here I go suffering a set-back.*

Liberty's Answer: There is a strong possibility that you have not known how to grieve for the loss of your father and then let God heal you. But there may be something else working here as well. Grieving over the death of a loved one is very appropriate, and God's own people, the Israelites, had a cultural tradition for grieving. If I remember right, many came to grieve with the Jewish family for several days, a few relatives stayed with them for up to a month, and then it was time to go on with their lives. Has anyone else shared any of their grief over your father's death with you?

David was devastated when his baby son by Bathsheba was deathly ill. But upon hearing the baby had died, David arose from seven days of fasting and praying, washed, dressed, went to worship God, and then ate a meal. He told his amazed palace staff, *"While the child was still alive, I fasted and wept. I thought, Who knows? The LORD may be gracious to me and let the child live. But now that he is dead, why should I fast? Can I bring him back again? I will go to him, but he will not return to me"* (2 Samuel 12:22-23, *NIV*). This sounds like a pretty fast recovery, but actually it was a strong faith in God and unwavering acceptance of His will that allowed David to move past his grief and back into life.

You say people have always viewed you as a really strong man. I suspect this was a facade you created to keep others from knowing that you were not that secure at all. I wonder if the overflow of feelings—the loneliness, rejection, despair, lost direction—weren't already corroding your soul before your father died.

My second book, ***Breaking the Power***, has a lot of useful information and prayers to pray about the unmet needs, unhealed hurts, and unresolved issues that most of us have packed around for years. We try to stuff the resulting feelings pushing up out of these toxic holes in our souls, creating alternate personality facades to show the world. But when something hard hits us, the entire masquerade falls apart, and the painful feelings gush out. I think this is where you are now.

Only when you begin to loose the strongholds rationalizing those old painful attitudes, wrong beliefs, and wrong ideas stored in your soul can God help you clean out the debris.

You need this cleansing work to let Him build a new foundation from which you can learn to trust and love others. You can grow into wholeness.

If some of your unresolved grief is tied into feeling guilty unless you are still feeling pain because your Dad is gone, then you need to pray and loose soul ties you may still be holding onto. These would have come from wrong agreements you are still believing—agreements such as your father being the only one who really cared about you. Perhaps you do not know whether or not he was saved. No human being on earth knows what kind of mortal conversation any dying person has had with Jesus Christ in their final seconds of life as we know it. You can hope that the Lord helped him accept Christ in the final moments. It is always right to hope that God's grace and mercy moved in and overwhelmed him. Seconds to us can become hours in the Lord's hands.

> **"Hope does not disappoint, because the love of God has been poured out in our hearts by the Holy Spirit who was given to us"**
> (Romans 5:4-5, *NKJV*).

Matthew Henry's Commentary, my favorite, says this about hope: "This hope maketh not ashamed; that is, it is a hope that will not deceive us. Nothing confounds more than disappointment. This hope will not disappoint us, because it is sealed with the Holy Spirit as a Spirit of love."

Hope for the love of God to have overwhelmed your Dad at the final second of his life if you do not know the state of his salvation. God has said our hope in Him will never disappoint or make us ashamed of having hoped. We will be praying for you.

3

Relationship with Marriage Partners

Question: *For years, I have carried the bulk of keeping my marriage going, and I am literally worn out with the stress of it all. I have not read your books, I just found your site on the internet. If I leave my spouse, will I ruin my chance of ever being used in ministry by God? My spouse is not saved, and I don't want to refuse to be used to help this to happen. But, I'm so discouraged about ever fulfilling my ministry calling.*

Liberty's Answer: I am sure you are exhausted from trying to carry something that your soul cannot carry, fix, or strengthen in its own power. Since you say you have not read any of my books, please consider getting at least the first book, ***Shattering Your Strongholds.*** This book has three major prayers in it that will help you get started in praying with the Keys of the Kingdom prayer principles (pages 131, 139, and 171). I would suggest you pray the first two for yourself every day, and pray the prayer on page 171 for your wife every day. Do this until you feel you are able to pray these prayer principles on your own. The prayer principles in these particular prayers are important guidelines to praying effectively—seeking God's will. Below are excerpts from these basic binding and loosing prayers:

> *"I bind my body, soul and spirit to the will and purposes of God for my life . . . to the truth of God . . . and to the awareness of the power of the blood of Jesus working in my life every day. I bind my mind to the mind of Christ that I can have the thoughts, purposes and feelings of His heart in me. I bind my feet to the paths you have ordained for me to walk, Lord. I repent of having wrong attitudes and thoughts, renounce them now,*

and ask your forgiveness. I loose wrong patterns of thinking, attitudes, ideas, desires, and beliefs from my soul. I tear down, crush, smash and destroy every stronghold I have erected to protect them. I loose the power and the effects of any harsh or hard words (word curses) *spoken about me, to me, or by me. I loose any strongholds in my soul protecting wrong feelings I have against anyone. Forgive me as I forgive those who have caused me pain, loss or grief. Amen.* " (page 131, *SYS*)

"In the name of Jesus Christ, I bind_____ 's body, soul, and spirit to the will and purposes of God for his/her life. I bind _____'s mind, will, and emotions to the will of God. I bind him/her to the truth. I bind his/her mind to the mind of Christ, that the very thoughts, feelings and purposes of His heart would be within his/her thoughts. I bind_____ 's feet to the paths of righteousness that his/her steps would be steady and sure. I bind him/her to the work of the cross with all of its mercy, grace, love, forgiveness and dying to self. I loose every old, wrong, ungodly pattern of thinking, attitude, idea, desire, belief, and

motivation from him/her. I loose the power and effects of deceptions and lies from him/her. I loose the confusion and blindness of the god of this world from _____ 's mind that has kept him/her from seeing the light of the gospel of Jesus Christ. Father, I crush, smash and destroy generational bondage thought patterns of any kind arising out of mistakes made at any point between generations. They will not bind and curse any more members of this family. Amen." (page 171, *SYS*)

These prayers will give you a new way of aligning yourself with God's will for your life and letting Him heal your soul. Pray the first one for yourself first, then pray the second one for your wife.

Regarding your ministry, the gifts of God are irrevocable and given without any taking back. However, your ability to express your ministry gifts with divine influence is not guaranteed. Especially if you are struggling with a hardening in your soul (heart). You have to be able to receive freely from God's Spirit to express His gifts purely.

If a major oil company gave you a wonderful car that only they knew how to fuel and maintain and they promised that they would, it would certainly behoove you to keep them involved in the upkeep of your new car. If you were unwilling to let them power and maintain your gift, it would be just a matter of time before you were pushing the car to get it anywhere. The wonderful gift would then become a burden to you. Gifts that require special power and maintenance should be brought before the original owner as often as necessary for their upkeep.

> ***Spiritual gifts that are not divinely influenced can quickly turn into soulish expressions with hidden agendas.***

Power, anointing, and gifts from God are always for service, never for status or approval.

Can a divorced person be mightily used of God? Yes. Is divorce a quick way out of a stressful marriage and into an anointed ministry? No. Divorce never clears your slate of unforgiveness, resentment, and bad feelings, in order to open doors of God-given ministry for you. Divorce always brings more baggage that must waded through. Divorce also tears at the credibility you would have with those who were struggling in their marriages. There certainly is life after divorce, but it takes a lot of prayer, a lot of dying to self, a lot of biting your tongue and swallowing blood, and a lot of loosing of stronghold thinking to find your ministry balance again.

However, <u>you are not divorced</u>. You are in a difficult marriage. You still have the opportunity of receiving help from God to see a miracle occur. I encourage you to seek His direction and guidance without allowing yourself to feel influenced by the "natural" human feelings you described. God will not hold mistakes against you that you have made in the past, if you truly repent of them, turn away from them and change. However, you may find the consequences of mistakes you make willfully from this point on much harder to overcome than you ever expected. Consequences come from every choice you make, some good, some bad. Willfulness makes the consequences considerably harder to get through.

I know you are discouraged and tired, but you can do all things through Christ which strengthens you. For Him to strengthen you and help you as soon as possible, He needs you emptied of your emotional and mental baggage. He wants you to be pliable in His hands— desiring His will. Your spouse's salvation is not your responsibility, it is His. However, divine love allowed to flow freely through a child of God will do whatever it can to help another person see how much God loves them.

You need to tell God that you want a paradigm shift in your thinking, and that you are going to stretch yourself toward it. That means you want to see everything in your life from God's perspective, not your own. He loves you both, and is reaching out to help you both. Draw upon His resources and hold steady while you begin to pray.

> *"Therefore, as the elect of God, holy and beloved, put on tender mercies, kindness, humility, meekness, longsuffering; bearing with one another, and forgiving one another, if anyone has a complaint against another; even as Christ forgave you, so you also must do. But above all these things put on love, which is the bond of perfection. And let the peace of God rule in your hearts, to which also you were called in one body; and be thankful"*
> (Colossians 3:12-16, *NKJV*).

Question: *We need prayer for our financial situation. We used credit cards to live on for several months while I went through a deep depression and* *was out of work. It has really affected our marriage because I feel my wife blames me for this financial burden. What can I do?*

Liberty's Answer: First of all, pray and bind your will to God's will in every area of your life. Pray the same thing for your wife. Then pray and bind both of your minds to the mind of Christ. After you do this, sit down and read your Bible for about 30 minutes. If you feel you don't have time to do that, then this is a foundational area that you need to reprioritize in your life. Read the Word slowly, with focus, savoring and concentrating on every word. Even if you do not read anything specific regarding provision and finances, the Word is incredibly multi-faceted and can be operating on any of the many layers of confusion and frustration you are both feeling right now.

Pray and ask God about what needs to be done to resolve and restore your financial situation. Again, bind yourself to God's will and commit your will to obeying whatever God says. Communicate how you are praying to your wife, but don't argue with anything she might say in response. Just tell her that you believe that God is the only one who can give the wisdom to navigate your way out of this indebtedness. Keep binding your will to God's will and your mind to the mind of Christ.

The lack of a job seems to be the major issue here, but it probably isn't. So, while getting a job may take some of the pressure off of the strain of your relationship with your mate, it won't resolve a lack of communication and issues between you.

> *"Remember this: he who sows sparingly and grudgingly will also reap sparingly and grudgingly, and he who sows generously and that blessings may come to someone, will also reap generously and with blessings"*
> (2 Corinthians 9:6, *Amplified*).

What have you sown into the intimacy of your marriage? It is hard to make yourself vulnerable enough to initiate intimacy when you are filled with walls of defensiveness and self-protection. It will be easier to sow love and the vulnerability of intimacy into your marriage as you let God get into the unhealed areas of your soul, and past the layers of your stronghold thinking, to begin healing you.

> *"God is able to make all grace (every favor and earthly blessing) come to*

> *you in abundance, so that you may*
> *always and under all circumstances*
> *and whatever the need, be self-*
> *sufficient—possessing enough to*
> *require no aid or support and*
> *furnished in abundance for every good*
> *work and charitable donation"*
> (2 Corinthians 9:8, *Amplified*).

Do you wonder why He hasn't done this for you? He is probably after something deeper in your soul. The lacking of finances may be the pressure He is using to get at the deeper problem. Do you think this could be that you do not trust God? Perhaps your job meant security to you, security that you controlled. I think this may be a fear of lack. The Lord appears to be allowing a turning up of the heat on both of you, and money has become a power issue between you and your wife. As long as both of you can believe that your problems stem from lack of money, then the lack of intimacy "issue" can be pushed down to a secondary issue. We will be praying with you

Question: *I became a Christian as a child, but I backslid and did not walk with God as I got older. I married at seventeen, ended up committing adultery,* *and then left my husband. During this separation, he divorced me. I began living with a new partner and that relationship also fell apart. By then, my ex-husband was completely unavailable for reconciliation. I have repented to God truly and rededicated my life to Him. I have since married my second partner who is now a born-again Christian. We have both repented of adultery and pre-marital sex. Will God honor our marriage, or am I bound to my first husband?*

Liberty's Answer: Your salvation and repentance wipes away the sin of your actions, but there may still be some hard consequences from them. You have every right to ask God for blessing and guidance and direction in accepting and learning from these consequences. Lean on Him with all your might as you do this, and remember that His grace and mercy are always available to the one who is trying to change for Him.

I believe you and your husband need to pray with great focus to loose the stronghold thinking in your souls. Unmet needs in the soul are always at the bottom of the drives that push people into getting involved in extra-marital experiences. If the unmet needs that first drove you to try to meet them have not been exposed to God's healing, they are still capable of pressuring you in the future. These drives are not things we can permanently control through will power. Your primary goal should be to open them up to God and let Him permanently meet them.

Cooperating with God as He supernaturally enables this cleansing and healing to take place will be much easier if you are loosing walls of self-protection and defensiveness. Fortunately, Jesus made it possible for us to cooperate with the dismantling of these protective walls. Your voluntary choice to do this because of a desire to be closer to God will ensure God's participation in the process. I'll be praying for you as you both pray this:

> *Lord, I bind my will, my mind, and my emotions to you. I want your will. I loose all wrong patterns of thinking, wrong agreements, and soul ties from my soul. Please pour grace, mercy, and healing into both my soul and my mate's soul. Amen.*

4

RELATIONSHIP WITH CHILDREN

Question: *My son is recently divorced. He believes that his wife was unfaithful and she believes that he was unfaithful. At the time neither one was, but she filed for divorce and it was final in August. He is now seeing someone else. Is it all right to bind him to his marriage vows? How would you pray?*

Liberty's Answer: Not knowing if they are saved or not, I would bind your son and his ex-wife to God's will. That places trust and confidence in God to work out His will in each of their lives, leaving the details to Him. I would bind both of them to the truth of the Word, and to an awareness of the power of the blood of Christ working in their lives. I would loose the effects and influences of wrong agreements from both of them, and I would loose wrong beliefs and ideas from their souls. I would ask God to pour out grace and mercy upon each of them.

I would declare that God's will would be done on earth in their lives, exactly as He has established it in heaven. I would agree with God's Word that says that the effectual and fervent prayer of a righteous man (or a righteous woman) would avail much. God's will can reign in this situation. He's looking for someone on earth to believe that He has a plan and then to agree with Him that it shall be done.

Question: *A friend and I are in disagreement over the following: I think if a parent is a strong Christian and prays in faith believing for the protection of his or her young child, then that child will be kept out of harm's way. My friend says that if a person is intent on harming that child, and the situation presents itself, then God cannot violate that person's choice to do harm to the child. My comment to that train of thought is, "Why even bother to pray in the first place?" Do you believe that a person can pray for protection for a child and expect God to honor that prayer?*

Liberty's Answer: Yes, I do. I also believe that when we bind our children to the will of God, God's will can easily override the working out of someone else's intent to harm them. God is so able to divert a stalker's attention (with a pit bull chasing him), to hide a child from view (the child gets swallowed up in a crowd), or to bring other people into the situation (a policeman's attention is diverted by an angelic act and he or she makes a wrong turn to show up suddenly in the wrong place at the right time). That stalker's will does not have to violated, it can just be baffled and bewildered! God can so mix up the factors in situations and cause them to play out according to His will without violating the willful intent of anyone else. Isn't that great?

Christian parents can have a lot of open doors in their souls because of unforgiveness, wrong agreements they have made, disobedience to God, etc. When these doors of access exist in peoples' souls, the individuals are open to spiritual attack in both the natural and in the spiritual realm. I also believe that their "believers" authority in Christ can be like Swiss cheese, because of all the open doors of access from their wrong thinking and stronghold building. I think this does place their children at somewhat of a risk.

Being a nominal or carnal Christian does not automatically endow a person with the same ability to access the authority of Christ and the power of God as the Christian who surrenders daily to God, obeys God's Word to the best of their ability, and wants God's will to be done on earth.

I'm not sure that the prayers of carnal, stronghold-filled parents have the same effect as the prayers of parents who are singularly focused on obedience and surrender to God's will. Before you decide that I am saying that some people's prayers could have more impact than others—maybe I am.

"For though by this time you ought to be teachers, you need some one to teach you again the first principles of God's word. You need milk, not s olid food; for every one who lives on milk is unskilled in the word of righteousness, for he is a child. But solid food is for the mature, for those who have their faculties trained by practice to distinguish good from evil" (Hebrews 5:12-6:1, *RSV*).

"Acknowledge and take to heart this day that the LORD is God in heaven above and on the earth below. There is no other. Keep his decrees and commands, which I am giving you today, so that it may go well with you and your children . . . ."
(Deuteronomy 4:39-40, *NIV*).

There are many Scriptures implying that when parents are obedient to the Lord, it will go well with them and their children. This certainly makes it imperative to realize that our lives do not impact only ourselves. So, if there is any possibility that how I live my life, how I surrender my self-will, how I obey God's decrees and commands, how I let go of unforgiveness and resentment—if there is any possibility that all of these things have an effect on my children—I'm going to live as right as I know how.

Question: *Our daughter, Tanya, is 27 and living at home with us. She has two small children born out of wedlock after a bad marriage. Since her divorce, I keep trying to convince her of the right things to do. About two weeks ago things started happening that appear to be connected to her former ways of thinking, but she keeps saying she has everything under control.*

I had bought your book on strongholds almost a year ago, but didn't finish reading it, in fact I loaned it to someone else.

*I got **Shattering Your Strongholds** back, read it and **Breaking the Power,** too. I have started praying over Tanya again the way you have shown in your book. I'm in so much pain with fear of things that are happening and need your advice. Since she is living in our home with her children, do I confront her on this, or is this my old nature trying to control the situation? That certainly is the way I have handled things in the past. Sometimes I get so angry at her. If you need more information, just ask.*

Liberty's Answer: No, I don't need more information. That is the beauty of these Keys of the Kingdom principles, details are not necessary to use them. Wanting God's will is what is important. First of all, you need to be praying the prayers in **Breaking the Power** for yourself, too! You are in a difficult situation for sure, but you cannot make Tanya change. You can, however, cooperate with God to cause yourself to change.

Have you been praying with faith in what good thing God will do, or are you praying to try to stave off your fear that He won't do something in time?

Faith in the original Greek (and most of the Hebrew) almost always goes back to the same basic meaning: <u>trust and confidence in the goodness and power and wisdom of God towards you and those you love</u>. Fear is a lack of trust and confidence in the goodness and power and wisdom of God, caused by emotional responses to unresolved issues out of your past.

Which frame of reference are you praying out of?

God loves your daughter more than you and your husband do. Do you believe that He is going to do what is best and right for her destiny purposes? Or do you think He is wringing His hands, wondering if you are going to pray loud enough and long enough?

1. **If you believe God loves your daughter more than you do, then you must believe that He can use His mighty power and great love to work for her good.**

2. **If you don't believe God loves her more than you do, then what do you expect Him to do in response to your praying?**

3. **If you trust that whatever He allows to come will be in her best interests, then**

45

**pray with gratitude. Thank Him that
you can come into agreement here on
earth with His great plans for her life
that have already been established in
heaven.**

**4.	If you don't trust God with your
daughter's welfare, then why pray at all?**

Concern, anxiety, stress, worry, and fear have never
caused God to change anything for good. Agreement
on earth that His goodness and power and wisdom in
the heavens will flow towards a loved one does cause
change on earth.

Iverna Tompkins used to say: "God will bring us
in on the easiest road we are willing to come in on."
When you pray the binding and loosing prayers, you
are praying in cooperation with God's workings in your
daughter's life. You are helping to clear the decks in
the spirit world so that the enemy has less and less ability
to manipulate her to rebel against God's workings.

One more tough question. Are you hoping that
your expression of fear and concern will influence
Tanya's choices? Saying this as gently as I can, that is
soulish manipulation. If Tanya modifies her behavior or
lifestyle because of your extreme fear and concern, it
will only be external and temporary. Any permanent

change has to happen inside of her. Praying the binding and loosing principles will help soften up her defense mechanisms and self-protection devices to open up a way for the Lord to get past her deepest strongholds.

God will not violate her defenses, except perhaps in the most extreme life threatening situations. But He will let her make choices that get her deeper and deeper into negative circumstances until she will finally surrender to Him voluntarily. Your focus must be to trust Him to be working everything together for good.

Let your outward demeanor towards her be a peaceful countenance, words of love and faith (not of preaching, not of warning, not of Scripture recitation), an attitude of patience (resting on the knowledge that God is working), and kindness (out of love, not to make her feel guilty). These spiritual manifestations are the fruit of the Spirit and they cannot be faked. They can only be manifested out of a heart that has decided God really is acting with goodness, wisdom, and power towards all involved.

Be sure and pray the binding and loosing prayers for yourself and your husband and your grandchildren as well. Be sure that you believe what you are praying—reinforce your belief by going back to Matthew 16:19 to reread what the Living Word said. Know that God has good intentions and plans and purposes for all of you beyond what you can see in the natural.

Speak right agreements about your daughter. Loose the effects and influences of all wrong agreements she has ever made, loose the effects and influences of all wrong agreements you and your husband may have made regarding her. Loose the effects and influences of all wrong, negative word (curses) you and anyone else (including her) have ever spoken about her. We will pray with you. Let us know about the changes.

> *"Do not be afraid, for I am with you; I will bring your children from the east and gather you from the west. I will say to the north, 'Give them up!' and to the south, 'Do not hold them back. Bring my sons from afar and my daughters from the ends of the earth—everyone who is called by my name, whom I created for my glory, whom I formed and made'"*
> (Isaiah 43:5-7, *NIV*).

> *"I will contend with those who contend with you, and your children I will save"*
> (Isaiah 49:25, *NIV*).

Question: *I have custody of and have been raising my five-year-old grand-daughter since she was a tiny baby. Her mother has visitation rights, but during times of visitation, my precious little grand-daughter has been molested, left unfed, unwashed, unsupervised, not dressed for the climate, plus more. I have read* **Shattering Your Strongholds** *and I am now reading* **Breaking The Power,** *and I pray for my little grand-daughter every night. But I worry about how can I pray most effectively. I know that one of my strongholds is a lack of complete trust in God. Another custody battle with her mother is coming up soon, so I'll be back in court. I'm so afraid of further pain to this child that I'm unable turn it over to God for more than a few frantic seconds.*

Liberty's Answer: Continue praying the prayers you have learned from these books. Insert your name, your grand-daughter's name, and the names of every person in this situation into every prayer that helps you release your frantic moments to God. Pray that God's will is done in the lives of everyone involved.

Loose the effects and influences of all wrong agreements made by your daughter, your grand-daughter, yourself, and every person in this situation. Loose the effects and influences of all wrong agreements made by other people about any of you. Keep asking God to guide you and give you direction. Bind any legal authorities involved in this situation to the will of God so that God's will is done on earth as He has already established it in heaven.

As you are praying for your grand-daughter, keep loosing any stronghold thinking that could be forming in her soul. Be very careful about what you say to her and around her. Do not speak word curses about her mother, and do not bring her into any wrong agreements because of your fears. Through your prayers of binding and loosing, you will be cooperating with His will being done on earth in this matter.

Question: *I just found you on the internet, and I feel good about what I have seen and read on your site. My son died over three years ago. The night he died, he was covered by the blood of Jesus and other prayers. But he died, anyway! He drowned, and I found him the next morning. According to prophetic words I have been given, he is in heaven. If so, then why do I hurt so much.? I don't understand death from God's point of view. I hope you can understand what I am trying to say.*

Liberty's Answer: I am so sorry for your loss. I don't understand death from God's point of view, either. We just have to trust Him and believe He will work things together for ultimate good. I would like to offer you the following prayer to pray, and I hope that it will bring you some comfort. Please pray this following prayer out loud, focusing on every word in it as you do. I will be praying for you, God bless you.

Jesus, I have lost someone dear to me. I feel such pain and grief in my soul right now. I also feel overwhelming anger, confusion, and fear. Anger because my loss is not fair. Confusion because I do not understand why. Fear because I don't know what else I might lose. Help me to surrender my questions and this unresolved issue to you and make room to receive your grace and comfort. I so need to make room in my pain and grief for your comfort.

I choose to embrace Christ's assurance that I will know joy, peace, and hope again. I choose to hold tight to your will for me as my life moves beyond this loss. I need your healing grace and mercy for my emotions. I bind myself to the truth that you will comfort and heal me, that you have plans and purposes for me beyond this time, and they are for good. I will not insist upon a question mark where you have placed a period.

I loose all thoughts of "if only I had . . . what if I had . . . why didn't I . . . . " I loose denial and hopelessness from my soul. I loose all ties my soul wants to keep to my son, and I choose to let go. I choose to recognize that healing will not mean I have forgotten, but that I will be able to think on the good memories with my son without an encounter with unresolved pain. I will not grieve over what could have been, rather I bind myself—body, soul, and spirit—to your good plans from this point forward in my life. Amen

5

RELATIONSHIP WITH RELATIVES

Question: *How should I pray for my sister who is on heavy medication for depression because her husband is cheating? She feels she can't read with all that is going on and the feelings she is experiencing. How can I help her?*

Liberty's Answer: I thank our merciful God that she has someone to pray for her and with her at this difficult time. Earnestly bind her mind to the mind of Christ, and loose the wrong thought patterns that are surely grinding through her mind. Particularly pray and loose the effects and influences of wrong agreements she has made. Try to get her to pray even part of the binding and loosing prayers herself.

Don't come into any negative, wrong agreements with her about her husband. You never de-victimize victims by agreeing with their victim status or agreeing with their beliefs about the horrible attributes of their victimizers. You help to de-victimize them by praying for them first, and then praying with them—praying words of peace, healing, mercy, grace and compassion.

> *Do not agree with negative prayers, any wrong patterns of thinking, or with any hopelessness she may express. To do so will only reinforce her negative feelings and beliefs.*

Try to think of ways you can avoid negative agreements without antagonizing her. She does need your compassion and support right now, but don't be a part of wrong conclusions that bring ungodly consequences.

As for praying for this husband, bind him to God's will. I do not recommend that you bind him to the marriage or to his wife. If he was not trying to make their relationship work before the affair, he may not yet be ready to try to make their relationship work now either. At least not until some godly changes occur in the souls involved. That is where you can begin to affect things from God's perspective.

Don't pray what <u>you think</u> Christ should be saying to her husband. Bind this man's emotions to the healing of the Holy Spirit. Loose soul ties from everyone involved. Loose wrong thinking from everyone who is involved. Don't curse or judge the other woman involved, instead pray and bind her to the will of God. Bind her mind to the mind of Christ.

Everyone involved in this tangled situation has unmet needs, unhealed hurts, and wrong thinking that God wants to meet and heal. Trying to force God's hand to enact judgment, through our prayers, is not our position or our right. It will rebound on the one who is praying such wrong prayers. Encourage your sister to come into right agreements with God's Word. Try to get her to agree by speaking Scriptures with you in agreement that God has not:

- **Left her or forsaken her.**
- **Lost track of her.**
- **Peversed His good plans and good purposes for her life.**
- **Ceased to want to use, fulfill, and bless her.**

Focus on praying that every person involved will be changed and healed, and that God's will (which is already established in heaven) would be done on earth from this point forward.

This is a terrible and painful situation for your sister right now, but there will be pain for everyone. God can use that pain to open up areas in the souls involved that might never have opened up voluntarily. Pray now in cooperation with God's will that what human souls have tangled up so badly, God will receive the glory for untangling it all in victory.

Question: *I began praying for a close family member a few days ago, and the next day he did something really dumb which resulted in the police arresting him. I am believing God will work this situation out, but I am worried. Is it a usual thing to pray the binding and loosing prayers for someone, and then have them manifest bad behavior in a manner that they never have before? This family member is a born-again Christian.*

Liberty's Answer: Yes, this is something that happens. God has been waiting for someone on earth to agree with His already established will and plans for this person to cause them to realize they are at a crossroads with His will. When you prayed the binding and loosing principles for him, you agreed with God's will for him. Now you have to let God accomplish His will in whatever way He sees fit. When God colors outside the lines of our preconceived understanding about Him, results will not always make sense to us. It is time to intensify your prayers of binding your will and your relative's will to the will of God.

Question: *Why can't my family see what God says He sees in me?*

Liberty's Answer: This unenthusiastic endorsement, "He's balding, skinny, and can dance a little bit," was the conclusion of those who watched the first audition of the great dancer/actor, Fred Astaire. Before so many outstanding peoples' value became obvious to all, their beginning achievements were often overlooked and even disdained.

There are many reasons why others cannot "afford" to see value in people around them, the chief one being that they feel they have so little value themselves. Unmet needs and unhealed hurt in other people can blind them to brilliance in those they desperately "need" to expect little from.

This can create a situation where the most valuable accomplishment in the world could be ignored. That is why <u>all of the efforts we put forth</u> to rise into our destiny purposes for God must not be tied to the approval of any mortal being. Your efforts for God must be influenced only by knowing that God says He has good plans and purposes for you (Jeremiah 29:11)!

Don't ever get into a performance mode of trying to be perfect to get approval from your family.

> *If that is the only time they ever show their approval, there is a deception in your thinking. Only your performance was approved—not you.*

Be kind, be helpful, be loving, and be focused on doing what you believe God would have you to do. But always know that being perfect (even if you could) won't guarantee their approval of you as a person. Bless their little unsurrendered souls, however, others can be very approving of us when our efforts have some kind of fringe benefits for them.

The world crucified the only truly perfect person who ever lived. He was so criticized by others, that every single thing He ever did upset someone. Still, that never influenced the choices He made to do God's will.

Criticism and lack of approval from your family does hurt, I know. But it cannot diminish what you do and who you are in God's plans—unless you choose to let it.

> *From God's frame of reference, He is quite assured that no one anywhere on planet earth is as perfectly endowed as you are to do what He created you to do!*

When you pray, bind your mind to the mind of Christ, and loose the stronghold thinking that your family should affirm you if they love you. You will have to also loose all expectations you ever had of their unconditional acceptance. Bind your will to the will of God, and loose the word curses (hard, negative words spoken to you and about you) and the effects and influences of wrong agreements that others have made.

And last, but not least, remember that in this world, success almost always comes easier to those who have relatives in high place. The closer the highly placed relative is to you, the higher you can go. <u>Don't fight the principle</u>! Just remember who your Highest Relative is—the one you call Father God. Go ahead, trade on His name!

Question: *How do I deal with family members who deny there if a difference in me since I've become a Christian? I know there have been changes, but my family members keep saying that I'm just the same old person no matter what I call myself.*

Liberty's Answer: Sometimes family members try to hold us at the level of our worst failures and weaknesses, don't they? It can be difficult for others when you have moved ahead with your life, and they haven't. If they feel unable to rise above their past, they may want to keep you rooted in your past as well.

Many learned people have said that you cannot change your family, you can only change yourself. I believe there are ways you can change your family's view of you. Just cooperate with God and keep changing your life.

> *You can always trust the power of a truly changed life to overcome anyone's reluctance to seeing that you aren't who you used to be.*

Especially when you are sure that you never make them feel worse about themselves. As you continue to change, and as you relax about how others view you while enjoying how God sees you, no one will be able to ignore the changes in you.

6

RELATIONSHIP WITH OTHER PEOPLE

Question: *I have finished reading **Shattering Your Strongholds, Breaking the Power**, and listening to your healing tape. I've been binding and loosing and things are happening. I know I am doing something right, but I feel confused. I have always had a lot of people reject my friendship, or reject me, I guess. Are my feelings of rejection and insecurity symptoms or strongholds?*

Liberty's Answer: Feelings of rejection and insecurity are symptoms of deeper sources—unmet needs, unhealed hurts, and unresolved issues. It isn't always important to know exactly which source is the cause, as they may even overlap. The important thing is to know that something has caused the symptoms you have mentioned, and God wants to heal it.

You need to pray with a deeper understanding of what you are doing. You are binding yourself body, soul, and spirit to the will of the Father, to the mind of Christ, and to the whole truth of God's Word. Focus on every word you are praying with the expectation that something is going to change within your soul to let God get deeper within its defense systems.

When you pray, "I bind my will to your will, God," are you just hoping His will is going to override your will and keep you from making wrong decisions? Or, are you believing that you are making your will align to His will?

When you pray, "I bind my mind to your mind, Christ," are you hoping that His thoughts will override your thoughts? Or, are you wanting to fix your thoughts on Him and stop reliving old thoughts, doubts, and judgments?

When you pray, "I loose stronghold thinking from my soul," do you really want to stop rationalizing your bad feelings about how other people have hurt you? Do you really want to stop denying that you are the one who has been holding yourself in this ongoing stronghold bondage?

These prayer principles will uncover all of these issues. But this is a good thing, because God can begin to heal this wrong thinking that has been clouding up your relationship with Him. Pray with faith and believe that God is working mightily as you are cooperating with Him.

Question: *I found your book a few months ago as I was preparing to teach about strongholds to my ladies' Bible study. Of course your title caught my eye, and after I had thumbed through and read bits and pieces of the book, I knew I was supposed to buy it. I have since bought your other two books and have almost finished the third in the series. I am so excited and thankful for your teaching. I have already seen changes in myself and I believe I am going to see changes in all of those I am praying for. How do you pray for so many people every day? I have almost 20 I'm praying for already, and the list is growing.*

Liberty's Answer: Sometimes I pray a corporate prayer for people, naming each individual as I pray. If I get an impression that I need to pray more specifically for one of them, I do so. I believe God is always faithful to point out those who need further prayer. I'm just extremely grateful that I finally feel my prayers about my difficult people, my difficult relationships, and my family members are the most effective they have ever been! Of course, these prayers are mightily working in me, too!

7

FINAL THOUGHTS

Put on your seat belt and prepare yourself to receive integrity in your Christian walk. In an old 1855 Webster's Dictionary, the word integrity is defined as "wholeness, the entire unimpaired state of anything, particularly of the mind." Personal integrity comes to you as an extension of being whole, of being unimpaired by former patterns of thinking that were forcefully impacting your actions and your feelings. This means you can finally:

> *"Let all bitterness and indignation and wrath (passion, rage, bad temper) and resentment (anger, animosity) and quarrelling (brawling, clamor, contention) and slander (evil speaking, abusive or blasphemous language) be banished from [me], with all malice (spite, ill will or baseness of any kind). And we can become useful and helpful and kind to one another, tenderhearted, compassionate, understanding, loving-hearted, forgiving one another readily and freely as God in Christ forgave us"*
> (Ephesians 4:31-32, *Amplified*).

People walk through life today with music thumping on their car radios, cell phones that seem to be surgically attached to their hands, and earphones from personal radios and CD players clamped over their ears. Does this not seem like a concerted effort of the enemy to so fill their minds with noise that they cannot hear the thoughts of the mind of Christ? As you bind their minds to His mind, they can make a choice to turn up the volume and block Him out. But before they make that choice, they might just hear part of what He is thinking about them. That's an exciting prospect!

A changed life, however—your life—will transcend any noise of the enemy.

The devil cannot blot out the power of a changed life!

So know that your God is wanting to work with you to make room for change in yourself, that you would pray with integrity (wholeness that is unimpaired) for others. That life change in you will not happen just because you try harder. If you trying harder to be perfect worked, why would you need God? We all need God very much, and I hope this book has given you some insight on how to work with Him instead of always being worked on by Him.

"To you who are ready for the truth, I say this: Love your enemies. Let them bring out the best in you, not the worst. When someone gives you a hard time, respond with the energies of prayer for that person . . . If someone takes unfair advantage of you, use the occasion to practice the servant life. No more tit-for-tat stuff. Live

generously. <u>Here is a simple rule of thumb for behavior: Ask yourself what you want people to do for you; then grab the initiative and do it for them!</u>

"If you only love the lovable, do you expect a pat on the back? Run-of-the-mill sinners do that. If you only help those who help you, do you expect a medal? Garden-variety sinners do that. If you only give for what you hope to get out of it, do you think that's charity? The stingiest of pawnbrokers does that. I tell you, love your enemies. Help and give without expecting a return. You'll never—I promise—regret it.

"Live out this God-created identity the way our Father lives towards us, generously and graciously, even when we're at our worst. Our Father is kind; you be kind. Don't pick on people, jump on their failures, criticize their faults—unless, of

course, you want the same treatment. Don't condemn those who are down; that hardness can boomerang. Be easy on people; you'll find life a lot easier. Give away your life; you'll find life given back, but not merely given back—given back with bonus and blessing. Giving, not getting, is the way. Generosity begets generosity"

(Luke 6:27-38, The *Message*).

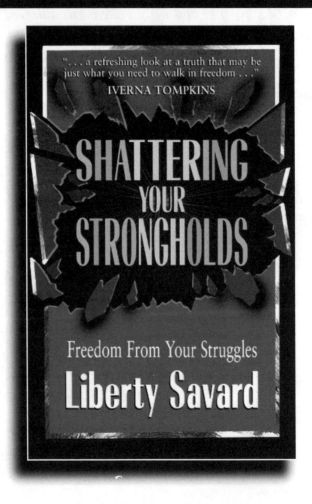

"... a refreshing look at a truth that may be just what you need to walk in freedom ..."

IVERNA TOMPKINS

SHATTERING YOUR STRONGHOLDS

Freedom From Your Struggles

Liberty Savard

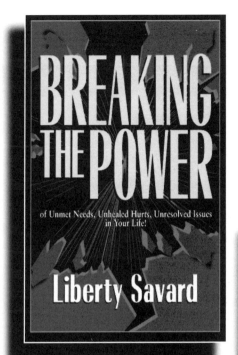

Liberty Says:

"The Keys of the Kingdom Binding & Loosing Prayer Principles are your means of bringing things on earth into alignment with God's already established will in Heaven"

Tapes & videos available. Shattering Your Strongholds and Breaking the Power also have accompanying workbooks.

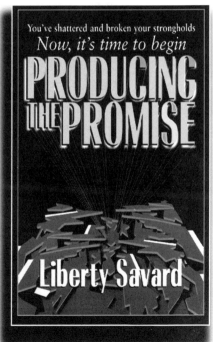